SINK YOUR TEETH INTO
SEA CREATURES

LOOK INSIDE THE JAWS OF

20

AQUATIC ANIMALS!

CONTENTS

OCEANS OF PREDATORS

Water: It's everywhere! In fact, oceans cover 70 percent of the planet. And those oceans are filled with life. We've discovered about 300,000 of these creatures, but we find hundreds more each year. Some people even estimate there are millions that we don't know about.

From the depths of the ocean to the surface of the water, the sea is full of fascinating animals that have all found amazing ways to survive. Many sea creatures are predators, preying on everything from tiny microscopic organisms to huge whales. There are razor-toothed sharks and fang-filled fish, gentle filter-feeding rays and giant baleen whales, toothed porpoises and beaked squid, and so many more.

With so many animals—and so many creatures to eat—you could say the sea is teeming with teeth! In this book, you'll learn all about 20 sea creatures, including how they live and what they eat, by peering inside their jaws. Turn the page to sink in!

SUPPERTIME IN THE SEA

FROM THE TINIEST MARINE ORGANISM LIKE PLANKTON TO THE BIGGEST BLUE WHALE, SEA CREATURES MAKE UP A HUGE FOOD CHAIN.

LEVEL 4

This is where the apex, or top, predators are. This includes lots of animals: fish like tuna, porpoises and toothed whales, birds like pelicans and penguins, and sharks, seals, and orcas.

LEVEL 3

Carnivores, or meat eaters, are everywhere in the ocean: Small fish like herring and sardines eat tiny zooplankton; larger creatures like octopuses eat crabs and lobsters; and big fish eat small fish.

LEVEL 2

In the next level, there are the herbivores, or plant-eating sea creatures. This also includes animals that eat that phytoplankton, like zooplankton, mollusks, and some jellyfish and other bony fish. But it also includes larger herbivores like green turtles and manatees.

LEVEL 1

At the bottom of the marine food chain are the little microscopic organisms like phytoplankton and bacteria that float in the water.

SINK YOUR TEETH INTO
SEA CREATURES

WHERE DO THESE TEETH COME FROM?
FIND OUT INSIDE!

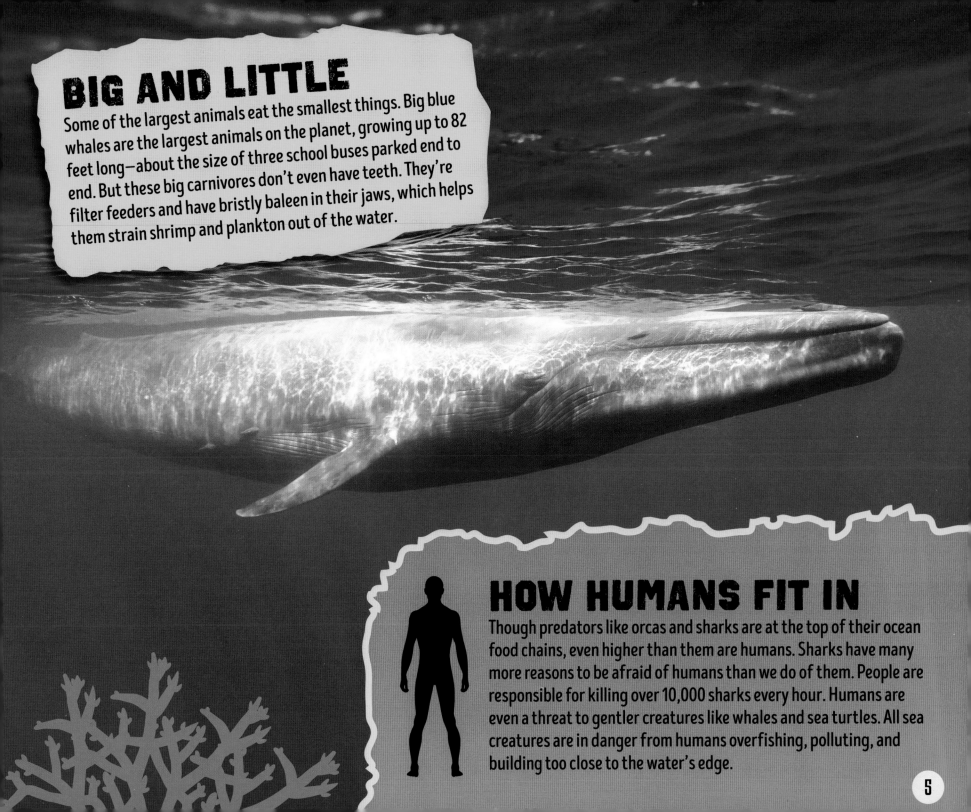

BIG AND LITTLE

Some of the largest animals eat the smallest things. Big blue whales are the largest animals on the planet, growing up to 82 feet long—about the size of three school buses parked end to end. But these big carnivores don't even have teeth. They're filter feeders and have bristly baleen in their jaws, which helps them strain shrimp and plankton out of the water.

HOW HUMANS FIT IN

Though predators like orcas and sharks are at the top of their ocean food chains, even higher than them are humans. Sharks have many more reasons to be afraid of humans than we do of them. People are responsible for killing over 10,000 sharks every hour. Humans are even a threat to gentler creatures like whales and sea turtles. All sea creatures are in danger from humans overfishing, polluting, and building too close to the water's edge.

ORCA

SCIENTIFIC NAME: *ORCINUS ORCA*

6 ft (1.82 m)

SIZE: Up to 33 ft (10 m)

LOCATION:
Oceans worldwide, especially in cold coastal waters

WEIGHT: 12,000 lbs (5,443 kg)

WOLVES OF THE SEA

They hunt in packs. They're apex predators. They use crafty hunting methods. It's no wonder that orcas are known as the wolves of the sea. Also called killer whales—even though they are a species of dolphin—these amazing creatures are incredibly deadly. Orcas have been observed actually tipping icebergs to get to a sea lion, or making waves with their tails to wash a penguin off some rocks—and into a waiting orca's mouth.

BITE MARK #1

Orcas are supreme hunters, and they'll eat almost anything. Walruses, sea lions, penguins, sharks, sea turtles—you name it. And they eat almost 500 pounds of food a day. With that kind of diet, you need some serious teeth. Orcas' 3-inch-long daggers are made for shredding. (Just check out the tooth that comes with this book!)

BLUNTNOSE SIXGILL SHARK

SCIENTIFIC NAME: *HEXANCHUS GRISEUS*

— 6 ft (1.82 m) —

SIZE: 16 ft (4.8 m)

LOCATION: Temperate and tropical waters worldwide

WEIGHT: 880 lbs (400 kg)

THESE SHARKS GO WAY BACK

These big sharks are part of the cow shark family, a group of modern-day sharks that look very much like fossils suggest some prehistoric sharks may have looked like in the Triassic Period 200 million years ago. This indicates they are built for survival. The bluntnose sixgill shark's name says a lot about it. Its rounded head and snout are blunt, and it has six gills rather than the usual five. During the day, sixgills live deep in the ocean, hanging out around 6,000 feet (1,829 m). But at night, they swim to the surface to feed.

BITE MARK #2

The bluntnose sixgill doesn't have many teeth, but it puts the ones it has to good use. There are just six teeth in the lower jaw, each sawlike one made up of little ridges that get smaller along the tooth. (Like one of the teeth that comes with this book!) They have nine pointier ones on the top jaw. The jaws come together for a powerful bite that's great for catching and sawing just about any fish or ray that cross its path.

BOTTLENOSE DOLPHIN

SCIENTIFIC NAME: *TURSIOPS TRUNCATUS*

6 ft (1.82 m)

SIZE: Up to 12.5 ft (3.8 m)

LOCATION:
Oceans worldwide, especially in coastal waters

WEIGHT: 500 lbs (226 kg)

UNDERSEA SONAR

Bottlenose dolphins are named for their long snouts, which they sometimes use to root around the seafloor. Some dolphins put sea sponges on their noses to protect them from cutting themselves on rocks or shells. They live in groups called pods, which have about 15 to 30 members. Dolphins use echolocation—like sonar—to find prey. To do this, they make clicking noises; the sound waves bounce off of creatures and back to the dolphins, which the dolphins can sense and use to track their prey.

BITE MARK #3

Behind their smiles, bottlenose dolphins have 72 to 104 cone-like teeth in their jaws. They use those pointy teeth to snatch prey but not for chewing. Instead, bottlenose dolphins gulp down their meals whole. Favorite foods include many types of fish, and squid, as well as crabs, shrimp, and other crustaceans.

MORAY EEL

SCIENTIFIC NAME: *GYMNOTHORAX FUNEBRIS*

6 ft (1.82 m)

LOCATION:
Southwest
Atlantic
Ocean

SIZE: Up to 8 ft (2.4 m)

WEIGHT: Up to 65 lbs (29 kg)

SNEAKY SEA SERPENTS

The green moray eel is the biggest kind of moray eel. They are often mistaken for sea serpents because of their size and their frightening features. These big eels like to coil up inside cracks and caves in coral reefs, and usually just poke their heads out to snag an unsuspecting squid as it slides by. Green moray eels are really brown, but they have a coating of yellow mucus on their bodies that make them look bright green.

BITE MARK #4

Green moray eels have long, spiny teeth, which are clearly on display every time the eels opens their mouths to breathe. Their strong teeth help them snare slippery prey like octopus and squid, which they attack by surprise at night. Morays also have a second set of jaws in their throat that move forward to help pull prey farther into their digestive system.

GREAT BARRACUDA

SCIENTIFIC NAME: SPHYRAENA BARRACUDA

6 ft (1.82 m)

SIZE: 4–5 ft (1.2–1.5 m)

LOCATION: Tropical waters worldwide

WEIGHT: 100 lbs (45.3 kg)

TIGERS OF THE SEA

Sometimes called the tigers of the sea, these big, toothed fish are like underwater torpedoes. Long, thin, and streamlined, they can swim at bursts of up to 35 miles per hour (56 kph). Barracudas rely on this speed, plus their keen eyesight, to track down food. They sometimes mistake shiny objects in the water for the flash of sun against a fish's scales, and they have been known to swim in and take a swipe at divers' metal tools, or shiny metal objects attached to boats.

BITE MARK #5

Barracudas have not one, but two rows of sharp teeth. The outer row is made up of small, saw-like teeth set close together. They help tear through prey. The inner set of teeth are long, spear-like ones that fit together when the barracuda closes its mouth. They trap prey and won't let it go. The two sets of teeth used together allow barracudas to break down big fish like grouper, snapper, and tuna into smaller chunks. Little fish like herrings and anchovies are swallowed in one gulp.

CROCODILE SHARK

SCIENTIFIC NAME: *PSEUDOCARCHARIAS KAMOHARAI*

6 ft (1.82 m)

SIZE: 2-3 ft (76-91 cm)

LOCATION: Tropical waters worldwide at depths of around 1,000 ft (300 m)

WEIGHT: 9-13 lbs (4-6 kg)

WHAT BIG EYES YOU HAVE!

You can't miss a crocodile shark's huge black eyes. These saucerlike peepers may help crocodile sharks hunt in the dark depths of the sea, allowing them to spot bioluminescence (or glowing light from other creatures) in the pitch black. Their name comes from the Japanese words *mizu wani*, or "water crocodile," a name fishermen probably gave to these sharks because of how much they snapped like a croc when caught.

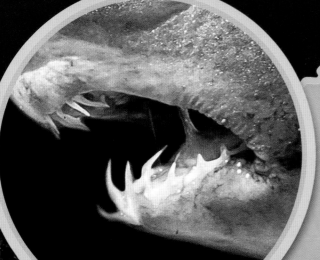

BITE MARK #6

The crocodile shark has teeth made for gripping. This deep-ocean shark needs them to grab and hold prey like bristlemouth fish and lanternfish. Shrimp and squid beaks have also been found in their stomachs.

SPERM WHALE

SCIENTIFIC NAME: PHYSETER MACROCEPHALUS

6 ft (1.82 m)

LOCATION:
Deep ocean
waters
worldwide

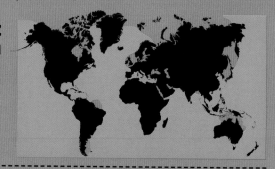

SIZE: 50-60 ft (15.2-18.2 m)

WEIGHT: 77,000-130,000 lbs (34,926-58,967 kg)

BIG BRAINS!

Sperm whales are huge: They're longer than a school bus. They also have large brains. In fact, they have the biggest brain of any known animal—living or fossil. A sperm whale's brain is five times bigger than a human's. So it makes sense that sperm whales also have a large noggin: Their head makes up one-third of the whole whale. It also houses a waxy material known as spermaceti. Scientists aren't sure what spermaceti does, but some think it helps the whale dive deep quickly.

BITE MARK #7

A colossal whale has a colossal appetite! These huge whales spend most of their time in the deep-sea waters, and so do the 45-foot-long colossal squid they like to eat. But sperm whales have narrow mouths and may not actually need their cone-shaped teeth for eating. Each tooth is about 3 to 8 inches (8-20 cm) long and can weigh 2 lbs (about 1 kg). Some scientists think sperm whales mostly use their teeth to fight other sperm whales.

MANTA RAY

SCIENTIFIC NAME: OMANTA BIROSTRIS

← 6 ft (1.82 m) →

WINGSPAN:
12–22 ft (3.5–7 m)

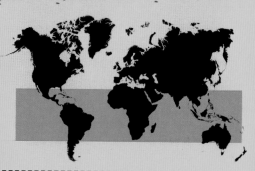

LOCATION:
Temperate
and tropical
oceans
worldwide

WEIGHT: 3,100 lbs (1,406 kg)

GRACEFUL GYMNASTS

These huge rays are called mantas after the Spanish word for blanket. Gentle and graceful, mantas look like they soar through the water with each flap of their huge wings. They can even turn underwater somersaults. Mantas have the biggest brains of any fish, and often seem curious about divers and boats. Each ray has a special pattern of spots that allows scientists to tell them apart, the same way that your fingerprints are unique to you. Though mantas are found in warm waters worldwide, they are being fished too often for their gill plates, and their numbers are vulnerable.

BITE MARK #8

Mantas are filter feeders. To feed, mantas simply open their mouths and swim. The water moves over their gill plates, which are five round filters that let water through but trap yummy plankton. Mantas eat 60 pounds (27 kg) of plankton every day. These rays have teeth, too, but scientists aren't sure what they use the 300 rows of teeny-tiny round bumps for.

GALAPAGOS SHARK

SCIENTIFIC NAME: CARCHARHINUS GALAPAGENSIS

6 ft (1.82 m)

SIZE: 12 ft (3.7 m)

LOCATION:
Tropical
waters
worldwide,
especially
near islands

WEIGHT: 189 lbs (85.5 kg)

ISLAND HUNTERS

The Galapagos shark was named after the islands where it was first spotted. Since then, they've been discovered off the shore of many other tropical paradises. With a big, round nose; long pectoral fins; round, beady eyes; and gray-and-white coloring, the Galapagos shark is usually confused with other species of reef shark. But these guys do have one unique trait, if you look carefully: There's a ridge down their back, near their back fin. When the Galapagos shark feels threatened, it will arch its back and hold its side fins down while swimming in a figure-eight pattern. If you don't heed this warning and back off, it will likely attack.

BITE MARK #9

Galapagos sharks feed mostly on animals that live on the sea floor, like rays, bony fish, crabs, shrimp, and octopuses. Their thin, pointy bottom teeth help them snare prey, while their large serrated, or jagged, top teeth help rip apart dinner.

HUMPBACK WHALE

SCIENTIFIC NAME: *MEGAPTERA NOVAEANGLIAE*

6 ft (1.82 m)

LOCATION: Oceans worldwide

SIZE: 45–50 ft (13.7–15.2 m)

WEIGHT: 50,000–80,000 lbs (22,680–36,287 kg)

TELL WHO'S WHO WITH FIN-ERPRINTS

Big, gentle humpback whales travel the world's oceans in small pods of two or three. They migrate—or move—more than any other animal, usually traveling about 3,000 miles (5,000 km) between locations. They feed in cool and polar oceans, and then mate and give birth in tropical water. Each humpback whale has a pattern on its tail that is one of a kind. Much like human fingerprints, whale tails help identify who's who.

BITE MARK #10

These big whales need big meals, but those meals are made up of thousands of tiny organisms. Humpbacks eat 3,000 pounds (1,360 kg) of food—small fish, krill, or plankton—every day. To do that, they take ginormous gulps of water—possible thanks to their ribbed, expandable throats—and then push the water through baleen. Baleen is made up of 200-400 brushlike plates that are about 30 inches (76 cm) long. The plates allow water to filter out while keeping the krill in so the whale can swallow the leftover food.

ELEPHANT SEAL

SCIENTIFIC NAME: MIROUNGA LEONINE (SOUTHERN)
MIROUNGA ANGUSTIROSTRIS (NORTHERN)

6 ft (1.82 m)

LOCATION: The Northern species lives along the Eastern Pacific Coast; the Southern species lives the freezing waters around the South Pole.

SIZE: 20 ft (6 m)

WEIGHT: 12,000 lbs 8,800 lbs (3,991 kg)

PACHYDERMS OF THE SEA

Northern and Southern elephant seals are different species, but they do share common traits. Also known as sea elephants, the male seals have two things in common with their namesake pachyderms. One is their huge size: They can grow to be more than 20 feet (6 m) long—longer than an African elephant. The other: They also have trunk-like snouts. It's called a proboscis, and the seals can blow it up like a balloon. This helps make their grunts and barks louder, so the sound carries further. It's helpful for males to have a booming voice, because they can live with groups of 30 or more female seals. The loud grunts help then communicate—and scare away any new male seals.

BITE MARK #11

Elephant seals seem to have small teeth compared to their big size. But don't let those tiny chompers (like the one that comes with the book) fool you. These big animals use them to catch the prey—such as sharks, squid, octopus, and flat fish—that they find on their dives. And those dives can be deep, because elephant seals can hold their breath for two hours! Elephant seals use their teeth as weapons for battle, too, scraping them across the bodies of opponents. Ouch!

BLACK DRAGONFISH

SCIENTIFIC NAME: *OIDIACANTHUS ATLANTICUS*

6 ft (1.82 m)

SIZE: 12–20 in (30–50 cm)

LOCATION: Temperate oceans in the southern hemisphere

WEIGHT: UNKNOWN

FISHING FOR FISH

Lurking in the 6,500-feet-deep (1.9-km-deep) waters are the fierce-looking black dragonfish, which come in two sizes. The females are large, growing up to 20 inches (50 cm) long. And they have gaping mouths, huge teeth, and chin barbels, which are long, rodlike body parts. The males are mini, usually growing less than 2 inches (5 cm) long, and they don't have teeth or even a digestive system. Another notable difference is that the females are actually black while the males are brown.

BITE MARK #12

Black dragonfish have long fangs, which they use to snare prey. They then open their mouths wide and gulp down their meal. The female dragonfish's chin barbel is tipped with glowing photophores. When wiggled back and forth in the dark water, the blinking light looks like prey, so fish swim up for a bite—only to end up in the jaws of the dragonfish.

LAMPREY

SCIENTIFIC NAME: *PETROMYZON MARINUS*

6 ft (1.82 m)

SIZE: 12–20 in (30–50 cm)

LOCATION: Northern and western Atlantic Ocean

WEIGHT: 8–13 lbs (3.6–5.9 kg)

BLOODSUCKERS

At first glance, a lamprey might look like an eel: It has a long, smooth tubelike body, with no noticeable scales, fins, or gills. But lampreys are indeed fish. Their bodies are made of cartilage, like sharks' bodies, which makes them flexible. This is important because lampreys aren't strong swimmers. Instead, they latch onto their prey and go for a ride. Lampreys have mouths like suckers, and they bite into a larger fish to feed on its blood. Though they live in the ocean, sea lampreys travel up freshwater rivers and streams to lay eggs.

BITE MARK #13

Sea lampreys' round mouths are ringed with hooklike teeth, which helps them attach to prey. They then use their rough tongues to lick away the fish's scales and skin, for direct access to the fish's blood. If the host fish is big enough, it will usually survive once the lamprey decides to let go.

COMMON FANGTOOTH

SCIENTIFIC NAME: *ANOPLOGASTER CORNUTA*

6 ft (1.82 m)

LOCATION: Temperate deep seas worldwide

SIZE: 7 in (18 cm)   **WEIGHT:** UNKNOWN

DANGER IN THE DARK

With its big head, big jaws, and big teeth, the common fangtooth is all about eating. But unlike most deep-sea creatures, this guy doesn't have any glowing bits or tricky lures to attract other fish to him. Instead, this serious hunter tracks prey using smell and possibly some sight, though in the dark, 9,562-foot-deep (2,915-meter-deep) waters it lives in, there's little light to help it see anything. Fangtooth fish have been known to swim in up to 442-foot-deep (135-meter-deep) water at night following food. Otherwise, not much is known about this mysterious deepwater creature.

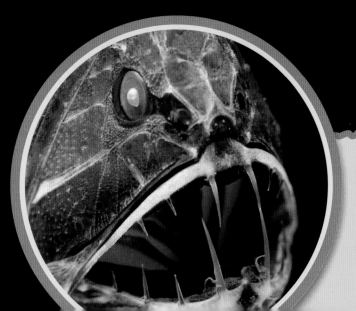

BITE MARK #14

Unlike other deep-sea fish, fangtooth fish aren't ambush hunters. That means that they chase down their food rather than hang out and wait for it to come by. So the fangtooth fish use their huge teeth for grabbing and holding on.

SLOANE'S VIPERFISH

SCIENTIFIC NAME: *CHAULIODUS SLOANI*

6 ft (1.82 m)

LOCATION:
Deep
temperate
waters
worldwide

SIZE: 11-12 in (28-36 cm)   **WEIGHT: UNKNOWN**

ALLURING LIGHTS

Not much is known about these freaky-looking fish, because they live very deep in the sea, about 3,280 to 6,561 feet (1,000-2,000 m) down. Very little light can reach these depths. So the viperfish use a little trick: Running along its sides, the viperfish has organs that light up in the dark. These little nightlights can lure in other fish, which think the lights are a yummy glowing bit of food to eat. Viperfish even have a small fin that sticks up, almost like a fishing pole, to help them fool prey, which end up in their terrifying jaws.

BITE MARK #15

Viperfish have fierce-looking jaws, with half-inch-long (1.3-cm-long) teeth poking out from them. Their lower jaw sticks out farther than the top, which helps the fish open their mouths wide to swallow prey, like other fish, whole. Viperfish have an expandable stomach, which means they have to eat only about once every 12 days.

LEATHERBACK TURTLE

SCIENTIFIC NAME: *ODERMOCHELYS CORIACEA*

6 ft (1.82 m)

SIZE: 7 ft (2 m)

LOCATION: Oceans worldwide

WEIGHT: More than 2,000 lbs (900 kg)

TOP TURTLES

These big sea turtles are named for their soft, blue-black shells, which are more like flexible leather than the hard material of other turtles' shells. If turtles had contests, leatherbacks would be winners. They are the biggest turtles in the word. They can dive deeper than any other turtle, hitting depths of 4,200 feet (1,280 m). And they are found all over the world—in more places than any other reptile. Even so, leatherbacks are endangered, and some groups from the Pacific Ocean have disappeared.

BITE MARK #16

Leatherback sea turtles eat only jellyfish, and to get as big as they do, they have to eat a lot of jellies. They have sharp pointed beaks, with razor-like sides for snipping prey. And their throats are filled with scary-looking spikes that face toward their stomach. This prevents slippery jellies from sliding out of their throats.

SALMON SHARK

SCIENTIFIC NAME: *OLAMNA DITROPIS*

6 ft (1.82 m)

SIZE: 10 ft (3 m)

LOCATION:
Cold North
Pacific
waters

WEIGHT: 992 lbs (450 kg)

GREAT WHITE LOOK-ALIKE

With its gray back and white belly, this large shark is often mistaken for a great white. But if you look closely, you'll spot some differences. The gray on the salmon shark is much darker than on a great white, and its snout is shorter. These fish swim in cold Pacific waters. Even though they get their name from the salmon—a fish that makes up a large part of their diet—they're known to feed on whatever they come across. They'll hunt trout, sardines, mackerel, lumpfishes, and anything else that likes the chilly water. They're also speedy sharks: Navy scientists found that they can zoom underwater at 50 miles per hour (80 kph).

BITE MARK #17

Salmon sharks have large knifelike teeth, with little mini teeth on each side of the larger ones. These special chompers help salmon sharks snare the quick-moving, bony fish they like to eat.

GIANT HUMBOLDT SQUID

SCIENTIFIC NAME: *DOSIDICUS GIGAS*

6 ft (1.82 m)

SIZE: 6 ft (1.8 m)

LOCATION: Pacific waters from Chile to California

WEIGHT: 100 lbs (50 kg)

ONE FLASHY SQUID

Even though they're not the biggest squid in the sea, Humboldt squid are sometimes called jumbo squid because of their size: Their mantle—or the main part of their body—can be as tall as a grown person, and their tentacles can grow another few feet. They're also nicknamed red devils, because they're tough and because they can change color from white to bright red and back. In fact, scientists discovered that Humboldt squid talk to each other by flashing quickly from red to white. If only we could figure out what they were trying to say, we could talk in squidspeak!

BITE MARK #18

Similar to other types of squid, Humboldt squid grab prey with their eight grasping arms covered in suckers. Then they use their two attack tentacles, spiked with pointy teeth-like barbs, which pull the prey toward their sharp beaks. A meal is usually fish or crustaceans.

OCEANIC WHITETIP SHARK

SCIENTIFIC NAME: *OCARCHARHINUS LONGIMANUS*

6 ft (1.82 m)

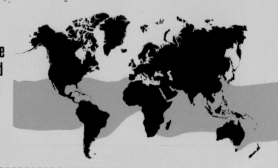

LOCATION: Far offshore tropical and subtropical waters worldwide

SIZE: 10 ft (3 m)

WEIGHT: 370 lbs (167 kg)

DANGER! DANGER!

Though these oceanic sharks cruise far offshore, away from where people swim and surf, they're still one of the deadliest sharks in terms of attacks on humans. Oceanic whitetips, well known for the markings on their rounded, paddle-like fins, are always the first to show up if there's a disaster at sea. During World War II, there were reports of hundreds of sailors and steamship passengers being attacked by whitetips after their ships were torpedoed. These days, though, humans are far more deadly to whitetips: Their numbers have dropped 70 percent in the years between 1969 and 2003.

BITE MARK #19

On the top jaw, these shark have triangular teeth for slicing. On the bottom, they have pointed ones for gripping. This makes them perfect predators for large, open-ocean fish like tuna, barracuda, and dolphinfish.

NARWHAL

SCIENTIFIC NAME: MONODON MONOCEROS

6 ft (1.82 m)

LOCATION:
Chilly arctic waters

SIZE: 15-20 ft (4.5-6 m)   WEIGHT: 3,000 lbs (1,360 kg)

UNICORNS OF THE SEA

Narwhals are porpoises. The males sport long tusks that can grow up to 9 feet (3 m) long. Females sometimes grow shorter tusks or have none, and some narwhals can grow two tusks. Narwhals usually travel in large groups of about 15, called pods, but people have reported seeing hundreds and even thousands meeting up at a time. These unique creatures live in Arctic seas and sometimes rivers.

BITE MARK #20

The narwhal's tusk is actually a long tooth. It grows through its top lip. The tusk contains tons of nerve endings, too. Exactly how narwhals use these crazy teeth has been a bit of a mystery. But recently, drone images revealed that narwhals use them to slash at arctic cod. It stuns the fish and makes them easier to eat.

PLAYING WITH THEIR FOOD

MEALTIME AT SEA ISN'T ALL SERIOUS HUNTING. SOME SEA CREATURES HAVE FOUND FUNNY WAYS TO GET THEIR FOOD.

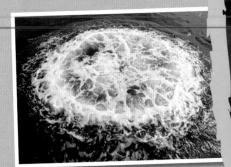

BUBBLE NET

BUBBLE TROUBLE

Humpback whales and dolphins have been observed creating bubble nets. They take a big gulp of air with their blowholes at the surface of the water before taking a deep dive. At the bottom of the sea, they swim in circles under their prey, releasing little bubbles as they go. This creates a funnel of bubbles, which confuses fish and krill and keeps them close together. The prey stay within the bubble net, which allows the whale or dolphin to swim up from below and gulp them down.

LOOPY LURES

Many deep-sea fish have strange body parts that act as fishing lines when they're wiggled around. Frogfishes, who live in shallower waters, also use this trick, coupled with a fantastic disguise. Frogfish have some of the best camouflage in the world, and it's hard to see the fish against a rock, coral, or seafloor. Well hidden, it dangles its lures—called esca—which look like two wriggling worms. A hungry fish will swim down to check it out, and the frogfish will strike out faster than any other creature in the world. If the frogfish happens to miss, and the fish makes off with its esca, no worries. The esca will grow back.

ESCA

KNOCK, KNOCK

Sea otters live and play in kelp forests, and they love to dine on shellfish and crustaceans. Though they do have sharp little teeth, they're often not enough to crack through a tough shell. To help, these crafty creatures get their paws on some tools. Otters will fetch a jagged rock from the seafloor, scoop up a tasty but prickly urchin, and then float on their backs while banging the urchin against the rock. When it finally cracks like an egg, the otter enjoys a tasty snack.

Brimming with creative inspiration, how-to projects, and useful information to enrich your everyday life, Quarto Knows is a favorite destination for those pursuing their interests and passions. Visit our site and dig deeper with our books into your area of interest: Quarto Creates, Quarto Cooks, Quarto Homes, Quarto Lives, Quarto Drives, Quarto Explores, Quarto Gifts, or Quarto Kids.

Sink Your Teeth into Sea Creatures is produced by becker&mayer! books, an imprint of The Quarto Group.
11120 NE 33rd Place, Suite 201
Bellevue, WA 98004
www.QuartoKnows.com

ISBN: 978-1-60380-410-3

Author: L. J. Tracosas
Designer: Megan Sugiyama
Editorial: Paul Ruditis & Meredith Mennitt
Image research: Farley Bookout
Production: Tom Miller
Product development: Peter Schumacher

MIX
Paper from responsible sources
FSC
www.fsc.org
FSC® C017606

Printed, manufactured, and assembled in Shenzhen, China, 11/17.

17 18 19 20 21   5 4 3 2 1

301921